PRIMARY
ADTEACHER'S
Pocketbook

By Bruce Potts

Cartoons:
Phil Hailstone

Published by:

Teachers' Pocketbooks
Laurel House, Station Approach,
Alresford, Hampshire SO24 9JH, UK
Tel: +44 (0)1962 735573
Fax: +44 (0)1962 733637
E-mail: sales@teacherspocketbooks.co.uk
Website: www.teacherspocketbooks.co.uk

*Teachers' Pocketbooks is an imprint of
Management Pocketbooks Ltd.*

Series Consultant: **Brin Best**.

This edition published 2004.
Reprinted 2007.

ISBN 978 1 903776 57 5

British Library Cataloguing-in-Publication
Data – A catalogue record for this book is
available from the British Library.

Design, typesetting and graphics by Efex Ltd.
Printed in UK.

Contents

Introduction

There can be no more important job in the world than providing our young people with the attitudes, skills and knowledge they will one day need to be fully functioning members of the society in which they live. Primary headship gives you the chance to do just that.

There is a great deal of literature out there which can tell you everything you need to know about all aspects of school leadership and management. This book does not aim to add to that; my intention is to give you a wealth of ideas to try in some of the different situations you will face during your time as a headteacher.

I have been fortunate in my life to have **enjoyed** 25 years of teaching (and learning) and this book gives me the opportunity to share what I have learnt with you.

Introduction

This book should help if you would like your school to be one where:

- Staff are motivated, enthusiastic members of a learning community who deliver outstanding learning opportunities to their children
- Children are leaping out of bed in the morning because they are just about to have **another** wonderful day in **your** school
- Parents work in genuine partnership with the school because they know that their children are truly loved, nurtured and will thrive whilst at the school
- Governors are an integral part of everything that goes on
- Standards (not just attainment levels) across and beyond the formal curriculum are constantly rising
- Everyone involved with the school **enjoys** what they do

In leadership
the journey is the
reward.

Establishing &
Maintaining
Credibility

 Good
Leadership &
Management

 Promoting &
Marketing your
School

 Efficient, Effective
Management
Systems

 Staff Welfare

 Motivating &
Energising Staff

 Improving
Teaching &
Learning

 Tips & Further
Information

Establishing & Maintaining Credibility

Establishing and maintaining credibility

When you take over and are expected to lead a school there will be a certain
level of expectation placed upon you by your new colleagues, the children, the parents
and the governors (as well as the LEA). Your personal credibility rating as judged by
them will have an enormous bearing on first, how you are perceived and second, how
willing everyone is to follow and support you.

You may bring with you a high level of credibility because you are already well known
in the area in which you work and your reputation precedes you. However, if you are
joining a school whose location is completely new to you, or where it is unlikely that
the existing staff have very much knowledge of your previous record, it's a different
story. You will need to pay a great deal of attention in your first year, and particularly
in your first term, to earning a level of credibility that will enable you to share your
vision and, subsequently, to achieve it **together**.

Credibility with everyone

There are certain things you can do which will help you to gain immediate credibility with everyone you meet:

- Pay particular attention to your appearance; think about what kind of image you want to create and create it!

- You may see the face that looks out at you from the mirror in the morning only once but it will be seen by everyone else that day. What kind of a face do you want everyone to see?

- Remember people's names and use them whenever you talk to them. For example, when you see Mrs Chand in the playground in the morning, rather than saying, *'Hello, how are you today?'* say, *'Hello Mrs Chand, how are you today?'*

Credibility with everyone

- Remember personal details about individuals and their families so that you can make reference to them when you next speak. When you remember these kinds of details about people you make them feel important

- Be everywhere (or at least create the perception that you are everywhere!) by being seen at crucial times before, during and after school – build in opportunities to be seen by committing space and time to your diary which ensures you will be at those places you've identified as important

- Live the message you espouse and model the behaviours you expect of those you lead

- Set the standard in **everything** you do and keep to it

Credibility with everyone

- Listen more than you talk – if you want people to support what you are trying to achieve, make them feel important by taking an interest and listening to what they say. Develop the skill of active listening

- Start each day positively and cheerfully – and stay there

- Seek the views of key stakeholders by introducing attitudinal questionnaires or suggestion boxes (or both) as a matter of course in the way you work and responding to whatever issues these raise

- Be more than punctual – arrive **before** you need to for all meetings, whoever they are with

- Happiness, humour and personal well-being are infectious – so SMILE!!

Credibility with staff

Successful leadership is less about **you** doing everything and more about you ensuring that everything that needs to be done gets done. So:

- Make a point of getting to know the names of all your staff within your first week

- Make a point of studying both the personal and the professional backgrounds of your teachers so you know what makes them tick and appear knowledgeable about them when you meet

- Call into teachers' work spaces informally as often as you can

- Greet staff personally when they arrive for work – use their names!

Credibility with staff

- Don't ask others to do what you wouldn't be prepared to do yourself

- Make sure your answer is always *'yes'* (although it may occasionally be *'yes, but not at the moment')* when a teacher needs to see you. Remember that they are restricted to non-teaching times to fit you in. If you can't see them there and then schedule an appointment for as soon as is practicably possible

- Be seen to teach in as many classes and in as many subjects as you can during your first six months. On every occasion do whatever it takes to make sure you deliver an outstanding lesson, but don't make a big deal of it yourself – the staff-room grapevine will do that for you!

Credibility with staff

- In all formal situations where you are seen by staff (staff meetings, whole-school assemblies etc) ensure that your preparation and presentation are outstanding

- Put a disproportionate amount of time into preparing your whole-school assemblies because they are (usually) seen by all the teaching staff and all the children

- Run an extra-curricular club (before you ask others to do the same)

Credibility with children

Children are the most important people in the school, so start as you mean to continue:

- Set up a school council and be seen to act quickly on the decisions it makes

- Ask the children what they most want in their play areas, and where possible provide it for them. Create a dynamic, imaginative play environment, allied to a positive behaviour management strategy (where the emphasis is on positive reward and encouragement rather than punishment and sanction) and watch the difference in the way the children respond to work and play

- Introduce 'trails' (maths, science, history, geography) around the school and its grounds – make the whole school the learning environment

Credibility with children

- All children love competitions. Introduce a range of competitions during the course of the school year, some of which run continually, some of which are occasional and others which are tied to subjects on the curriculum

- Spend one lunchtime each week with the children, joining in with their activities

- When reprimanding children avoid humiliating or embarrassing them in front of their friends

Credibility with children

- Pay compliments to children (especially the ones who have a reputation for bad behaviour) about their work, their behaviour, their appearance, so paying in to their 'emotional bank'. This is right to do in itself but it will come in especially handy when the time comes to reprimand a particular child

- Whatever you don't challenge you condone, so challenge every incident of unacceptable conduct wherever and whenever it takes place

- Create reward and recognition systems for children which operate consistently across the school

- Create an open door policy for children so they know that you are there for them. Let them know that nothing in the school is more important to you than them and that they can always come to see you if they need to

- Don't shout – try to deal with every situation calmly, fairly and consistently

Credibility with children

Milestone Celebrations

Introduce a range of 'Milestone Celebrations' which recognize and celebrate when children reach significant milestones in their school lives, eg:

- First week in school
- The day I became a writer
- The day I was told I could write in pen from now on
- The day I achieved the gold award for knowing all my times tables

There are endless possibilities, but you need to agree a protocol for how things are administered. Whatever you agree, each milestone celebration should culminate in some kind of presentation in an assembly to which parents are invited. Follow up with a permanent display of the milestone achieved, eg a Hall of Fame photo gallery (perhaps of all the children who know their times tables) which stays up until the child leaves the school. Have enough different milestone celebrations so that whatever particular aptitudes children have they are recognized. Every child needs to know that they will achieve at least one milestone while at the school.

Credibility with parents

Children's success in school is heavily influenced by a positive home-school relationship

- Introduce a workshop-style parents' meeting for all new parents where they generate thoughts and ideas about what they most want for their children during the next few years in your school. Follow this up with annual attitudinal surveys which seek parents' views on how successfully the school is fulfilling the wishes identified at that first meeting

- Keep a space in your diary from 8.45am to 9.15am every Monday morning and 3.00pm to 3.30pm every Friday afternoon when you are available to see parents on an ad hoc basis, should the need arise. Let all staff know that this is a time for parents and no one else

Credibility with parents

- When a parent telephones to make an appointment, try to agree to meet when it is convenient for *them*, and as soon as is practicably possible

- When a parent contacts you with a concern about their child follow it up **immediately** and get back to them that day to tell them the outcome. This is especially important if a parent is concerned about bullying, in which case drop everything and deal with it **now**. There is nothing so traumatic for a parent as the worry that their child is being bullied. Be seen to have dealt with it promptly and fairly in accordance with your school's anti-bullying policy

- Always return parents' phone calls the same day

Credibility with parents

- Before a meeting with parents find out as much up to date information as you can about their child/children, both in relation to school work and to their lives outside school. This way you appear knowledgeable about their circumstances and give the impression that you know and care about their child

- Be seen in the playground at least once a week before school and the same after school (more often if you can) and don't wait for parents to approach *you*. Remember, they are on your home territory so it's up to you to approach *them* to begin a conversation. Try not to go to the same parents each time as this may generate the impression that you have 'favourites'

- When in the playground before or after school make a point of talking to children. Be seen to be interested, caring and friendly with them – the parents' grapevine will do the rest!

Credibility with parents

- Develop a positive relationship with your local newspaper and ensure that every good thing of note your school does gets into it, accompanied by lots of pictures of children and their achievements. Parents' perceptions of the school change dramatically when they see their own children in the news

- Identify one significant, but highly visual, project which you can start and finish in your first term in the school and which is likely to be seen by all the parents. For example, redesign the school's main entrance for more visual impact, or embark on a transformation of the children's play facilities in the playground

- Play a full and active part in the PTA, attending as many of the functions as you can and circulating as widely as possible during the events themselves

Credibility with governors

The governors will be looking out to see what kind of appointment they have made. For many of them the only contact they have with the school is through the regular meetings. So:

- Have a long first meeting with the chair of governors to identify a *modus operandi* for the way you both agree you would like the governing body to function. Present your agreed expectations clearly and accessibly in the form of a school 'Governors' Handbook' (see page 72)

- Produce a highly organised governors' file with sections for all their documentation such as governors' handbook, minutes, agendas, school improvement plan etc. Present this at the first governors' meeting and explain how you envisage its use

Credibility with governors

- At the final governors' meeting of the year agree **all** the dates for the following year's meetings and circulate them to all concerned

- Make sure all information for governors is sent out well before the meeting and is of the highest possible quality. Avoid jargon, and where possible use graphs, charts, photos and other visual images, rather than pages of text

- Produce an attractive and colourful financial report format (use Excel) which is easily understood by all governors, especially those who do not have any financial experience

- Telephone each governor once a term (at least) to discuss how things are going. They'll be impressed that you took the time

Credibility with governors

- Develop a system to formally invite governors in for important occasions and events rather than 'hoping for the best'. Don't assume that because details of your events were in the headteacher's report or the school newsletter that governors will have seen it and made a note of it

- Ensure that refreshments are always provided before the start of meetings

- Try to be available for the fifteen minutes before meetings so that you can chat with governors as they arrive. You will need to make time in your diary to do this

Great leadership and management is less about doing everything yourself and more about making sure that everything that needs doing gets done.

Establishing & Maintaining Credibility

 Good Leadership & Management

 Promoting & Marketing your School

 Efficient, Effective Management Systems

 Staff Welfare

 Motivating & Energising Staff

 Improving Teaching & Learning

 Tips & Further Information

Good Leadership & Management

So what is good leadership?

A great deal of research has been carried out into what constitutes good school leadership. There are a number of key principles. Great leaders:

- Lead by example and model the behaviours they expect of others
- Have a clear philosophy and a vision which they share with everyone
- Understand the importance of delegation and empowerment, creating an environment in which there is shared leadership
- Have very good interpersonal skills
- Create learning communities
- Are calm but decisive
- Are prepared to take risks
- Have a sense of humour

So what is good management?

- Manage yourself before you manage others. Create good systems for yourself so that you are free to manage others
- Establish efficient and effective systems and procedures across the school
- Establish clearly defined roles and responsibilities for all staff and create concise job descriptions
- Publicise everyone's roles and responsibilities in the staffroom
- Spend time developing efficient and effective communication systems
- Remember – your teachers are people first and teachers second, so look after their personal needs as well as their professional needs
- **_Only do what only you can do!_** You may not feel able to follow this advice in your first year of headship, but once you have good systems and procedures in place you will find it easier

Who's got the map?
Being the strategic visionary

Once established in your school, it's important to remind yourself that although you want your vision to be delivered, you can't deliver it **all** yourself. Your role is to be the strategic visionary, to lead and empower your staff to:

> do things they don't believe they can do,
>
> achieve things they don't believe are achievable,
>
> succeed where success seems out of reach

...and then give them the opportunities and support to do it!

Who's got the map?
Being the strategic visionary

Vision without action = daydream

Action without vision = chaos

Who's got the map?
Being the strategic visionary

Creating your vision

Although your vision statement will reflect what you believe to be important in your school, there are a number of key principles to be aware of when creating it:

- Your vision is to be read by a wide-ranging audience, so use simple, unambiguous language
- Avoid the use of abbreviations, acronyms and jargon
- Try to use unconditional language, so rather than:

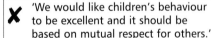
✗ 'We would like children's behaviour to be excellent and it should be based on mutual respect for others.'

say:

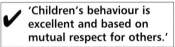
✔ **'Children's behaviour is excellent and based on mutual respect for others.'**

Remember this is a vision of how it is going to be not how it **might** be.

Who's got the map?
Being the strategic visionary

Creating your vision

- Keep it to one page of A4 if possible
- Try to avoid statements that don't mean anything such as, *'Every child to reach their full potential'*. What, before the age of 11? Now that would be something. Better to say, *'Recognise that every child has particular abilities and aptitudes and every one of them will have the opportunity to develop them here in our school'*
- Place a copy of the vision statement where it will act as a constant reminder to everyone of what the school stands for, eg school brochure, school improvement plan, governors' annual report to parents, entrance hall, staff notice board etc

Being the strategic visionary means constantly reminding yourself and others about where it is you're going and not allowing people to be deflected from it.

Make it happen – bring the vision to life

Once you have formulated your vision, remember it will only happen if
a) others share it and b) it is brought to life and kept alive at all times.
There are a number of things you can do to achieve this.

Share the vision by:

- Modelling all aspects of the vision statement in the way you and your Senior
  Management Team conduct yourselves at all times

- Re-presenting it to staff after one term and giving everyone an opportunity to
  discuss all aspects of it and say what they think. Be prepared to make changes to
  it in order to take account of people's views. This will help everyone feel a sense
  of ownership

- Placing a copy of your vision statement in a highly visible location in the staffroom where it is likely to be seen by staff **every day**

Make it happen – bring the vision to life

Bring the vision to life by:

- Producing (professionally, on long lasting, high quality materials) a 'School Charter' which sets out in clear, unambiguous and jargon-free language the key aspirations of the vision statement. Place copies all round the school where they can be seen by parents, children and staff

- Reminding staff about key aspects of the new, shared vision by placing statements from it as a header on staff meeting agendas. For example, from September to October half term every staff meeting agenda might have at its head the statement, *'Children's needs are at the heart of every decision we make'*. This is an overt, obvious reminder to staff of what you all value. Do the same thing on governors' meeting agendas

- Taking time to explain to the children, in language they understand, what the key principles mean. Be especially sure those children who are members of the school council have a clear understanding

Leading by example

If you really want people to deliver your shared vision, you will need to be aware that successful schools become a reflection of their leaders and that you need to lead by example in **everything you do**.

Try to remember that although you have contact with hundreds of different people each week, for many of those people that is their **only** contact with you and they will remember everything about it! Judgements will be made about you and your school based on that one single contact.

Leading by example

Some of the things you can do are to:

- Model the behaviours you expect of others
- Be seen to live the message and walk the talk
- Don't expect others to do what you wouldn't be prepared to do yourself
- Set yourself high standards of dress, punctuality, availability, approachability and presentation (especially in public situations like assemblies, Harvest Festival, Christmas events, PTA events, etc) and aim to maintain these standards at all times. You can't have high expectations of others if you don't have high expectations of yourself
- Treat **everyone** with respect, especially in the way you talk to them and even more especially in situations where others will see you

Everyone's a leader!

In order for your vision to be realised it is important to accept that it is not you alone who will be delivering it – it will be everyone working in the school. You have to demonstrate real belief in all your staff by giving them the opportunity to develop leadership skills so that they can deliver their part of the vision.

You can do this by:

- Meeting with **every** member of staff individually in your first term to identify their interests and particular strengths
- Agreeing a small (or not so small) project for each member of staff which will lead to them achieving some success early on and so create high motivation and self-esteem in the first few months of your leadership
- Recognising, rewarding and celebrating the achievements of every individual
- Providing training on leadership skills for everyone if you feel that will help

Delegation and trust

Once you have established yourself and earned credibility with
your staff there will come a time when you feel ready to
delegate key important tasks to others.

**If you want someone to do
a good job – give them a
good job to do.**

Delegation and trust

When delegating it is important to remember some key principles to ensure that your delegation strategy works.

Principle 1
You will have three kinds of people on your staff to consider:

The life enhancers

The lawn mowers

The well poisoners

Each of these types will bring different gifts to the party so think carefully about the characteristics of the individual to whom you are delegating before actually doing so.

Delegation and trust

Principle 1: Life enhancers

- Are often dynamic and inspirational
- See the good in every situation
- Get on with it and don't waste time – theirs or others'
- Will always find a way for things to be done – they have a 'can do' mentality
- Always seem to have more time than anyone else
- Create a feeling of well-being in others around them
- Can be relied upon to deliver
- Never find anything too much trouble
- Create positive energy
- Speak and behave positively
- Embrace change and take new challenges in their stride
- Infect others with their enthusiasm and passion
- Are high achievers, regularly achieving exceptional outcomes

Delegation and trust

Principle 1: Lawn mowers

- Work hard to do the right thing
- Care deeply about their roles and responsibilities
- Try not to let others down but sometimes find the pressure difficult to cope with
- Tend to be consistent, effective workers
- Occasionally achieve exceptional outcomes
- Sometimes find new challenges a threat
- Don't always cope well with change
- Are steady and dependable colleagues
- Neither create nor sap others' energy
- Tend to be functional without being inspirational
- Are prepared to accept new ideas if the argument is persuasive enough

Delegation and trust

Principle 1: Well poisoners

- Create negative energy around them
- Can always see reasons why something *shouldn't* be done
- Sap the energy of others
- Damage morale
- Offend others with their lack of commitment
- Regularly let people down
- Rarely deliver the goods, but find dozens of reasons why they didn't
- Blame others when things go wrong
- Seem always to be busy but never to be doing anything!
- Undermine their colleagues
- Can't see the point of change
- Tend to think they already have all the answers
- Upset staff, parents, children and governors with their insensitivity

Delegation and trust

Principle 2

Choosing the right person for the job is crucial to ensuring the right outcome. The person to whom you delegate an important task or project should be someone who:

- Genuinely shares the vision
- Has the motivation
- Has the skills
- Understands the requirements
- Is prepared to do what is required
- **Will** deliver on time and to the standard required

Delegation and trust

Principle 3

And finally, whenever you delegate a task you have to accept that the person who is going to deliver the goods will bring their own ideas, initiative and creativity to the task, so adopt the 80/20 principle to delegation. That is:

> If you end up with 80% of what you envisaged in the first place, be happy and celebrate the achievement.

It's very unlikely that everything you delegate will be done **exactly** as you hoped but if you get hung up on this, you'll find yourself thinking, *'If you want something done properly you have to do it yourself'* – and then you're on the road to exhaustion and burnout!

Two ears, one mouth!
Listen more than you talk

It was Dale Carnegie who said:

> 'Sit down with someone for five minutes and talk about yourself and you'll have a friend for five minutes. Sit down with someone for five minutes and let them talk to you about themselves and you'll have a friend for life.'

The most effective headteachers are those who realise that they don't have all the answers and are prepared to listen and take account of the ideas, initiatives and suggestions of others within the school.

Two ears, one mouth!
Listen more than you talk

There are a number of things you can do to become a good listener but, more importantly, to be perceived by others as a good listener:

- In all meeting situations ask others what they think about something before telling them what you think. Use language such as, *'What do you think of...'*, *'How do you feel about...'*, *'When do you think would be best to...'*
- Use affirmative and positive language when listening to others, eg *'I like the sound of that'*, *'That's a great idea'*, *'I think that may really work'*
- Don't just listen to the ideas of others, be seen to have acted on their ideas
- Don't interrupt!
- Structure staff meetings so that everyone has the opportunity to contribute
- Ensure that **every** member of the staff has a regular forum where they are able to say what they think in the knowledge that their feelings **will** get back to you and that you will act upon what you have learned

Two ears, one mouth!
Listen more than you talk

- Allow your teachers to tell you what you already know! Manipulate (in a positive, supportive way, of course) your meetings so that the new idea comes from them, rather than you!
- Steer them to tell you what you wanted them to say in the first place
- Develop **proactive** questioning skills
- Develop **active** listening skills
- Develop **empathetic** responses
- Try to avoid talking about yourself!
- Be aware of the importance of voice and body language in communication

Mind your language!
The importance of positive language

'Any fool can criticise, condemn and complain – and most fools do.'

Benjamin Franklin

Mind your language!
The importance of positive language

Creating a culture in which everyone uses positive language is the necessary precursor to achieving positive behaviour and to creating a sense of purpose and will to achieve. It starts with you and your SMT and spreads throughout your staff to the children. So:

- Change 'if' to 'when' and 'can't' to 'can't yet'
- Make positive comments publicly and negative comments privately
- Remind people of the **benefits** of what they're doing rather than the features of it
- In all feedback of any kind to children or staff use three positives to one negative
- Notice what people (children **and** staff) do that is pleasing and tell them – every day
- If criticism is necessary, try to get the individual concerned to make the criticism themselves.   Use language like, *'So how do you feel it went?'*, or, *'What do you think were the three best things and the one worst thing…?'* Usually, we know when we haven't done well, and it feels better if we recognise it ourselves than if someone else tells us. We're also more likely to be successful next time!

Risk-taking and innovation

Vibrant, successful schools are characterised by the fact that they do things differently from other schools. They are also led by heads and deputies who are innovative, creative and prepared to take risks. Don't be afraid to take a few chances in order to achieve your goal.

There are a thousand and one things you could do but here are a few ideas for starters:

- Make **all** learning multi-sensory
- Focus more on **achievement** and less on **attainment**
- Set targets in music, PE, the arts and humanities, not just in the core subjects
- Make your school an extended school open from 8.00am in the morning until 10.00pm at night to make it a real community facility
- Rewrite your schemes of work to make them fully cross-curricular
- Allow no child to leave your school without leaving a permanent, visible impression of their time there, perhaps through art, photography, sculpture or writing

Risk-taking and innovation

- **Don't** ban the things children like to do such as playing conkers in the autumn. Instead agree a protocol for how they **can** play conkers safely and without incident, then let them get on with it
- Build a 'stage' area in the playground, preferably a raised platform, where children can act, sing or work on their latest pop dance act!
- Organise a skateboard club which culminates in a competition at the end of term
- To improve attendance, organise a prize draw each month. Every child who's at school is automatically entered but don't tell them on which day it's going to be held. Award 20 prizes each time but make sure they're evenly spread around the school. (You may have to manipulate this a bit!)
- Hold a week long Arts Festival at the end of the school year and leave all displays up for September. Everyone enjoys the festival and staff just **love** the idea of not having to put up displays as soon as they return from the summer break

There's no end to what you can do to make your school different and special. But whatever you do don't be mainstream, conventional or conformist. **Be bold!**

Establishing &
Maintaining
Credibility

 Good
Leadership &
Management

 Promoting &
Marketing your
School

 Efficient, Effective
Management
Systems

 Staff Welfare

 Motivating &
Energising Staff

 Improving
Teaching &
Learning

 Tips & Further
Information

Promoting & Marketing your School

The school brochure

Your school brochure is very often the first thing prospective parents will see, often long before they meet you or visit the school, so it is important that the brochure itself is a true reflection of your school and its philosophy.

If you have inherited an existing brochure and you don't feel it accurately represents the direction in which you are trying to take the school, then change it.

When putting together your new brochure try to:

- Use the design skills of someone who knows what they're doing rather than do it yourself if this is not your strength
- Make sure the overall style and design reflects your philosophy. For example, if you believe wholeheartedly in the importance of creativity, innovation, the broad curriculum and the importance of sport and the arts, is that the impression a new parent would get when they see your brochure? Or is the design dull, mainstream, conventional and boring?

The school brochure

- Keep text to a minimum and break up every page so that no one page is just text
- Include plenty of illustrations and photographs of children involved in a range of activities
- If a particular point can be made graphically rather than with text then do it that way
- Don't be too flashy – many parents will feel that you are wasting school money instead of spending it on children's education!
- Keep the core information in the main brochure but have a pull-out section for information which is updated every year
- Think about the literacy levels of your parent audience and take this into account when producing the information pages

Visibility in the local and wider community

The best way to create a positive perception of your school in the local and wider community is to ensure that every positive event or activity involving the school is reported in the local media.

- Identify one person on the school staff (probably your deputy or assistant headteacher) who will have responsibility for promoting the school in this way
- Create some kind of communication network which guarantees that every noteworthy achievement of the school is notified to the nominated person

Visibility in the local and wider community

- Find out what the major festivals, celebrations and events are that occur in your community and look for ways that your children can be represented at all of them
- Try to exhibit children's art or DT work in local shop windows or entrance halls
- Display the school brochure in local libraries, surgeries and waiting rooms
- Make sure your children play a full part in the 'town' sports or arts events and be seen at these yourself
- Pay occasional informal visits yourself to things like the local WI meetings, pre-school playgroup AGM, presentation night at the end of the football season for the local junior soccer team (where you could offer to present one of the awards) etc

It is difficult to give more specific examples because every community is different. The important thing to remember is that the more frequently you or your children are seen in a positive light in the local and wider community the better it will be for the reputation of the school.

First impressions – the school entrance

Visitors to your school begin to form their first impressions when they enter
the premises and approach the main entrance. Put yourself in their shoes: go outside
and enter the school as if you were a prospective new parent.

Well, what impression do you think
the entrance gives?

First impressions – the school entrance

So, now you're in the shoes of a visitor, ask yourself these questions:

- Is the school sign prominently displayed at the main entrance and can it be seen well before anyone arrives at the school?
- Upon entering the premises is it obvious where I should park?
- Is the main entrance/reception clearly signposted?
- Does the entrance provide disabled/wheelchair access?
- Is the entrance to the school attractive and well maintained, or is the paintwork peeling and the glass covered in posters and advertising literature? If you feel you need to display important information for parents or other visitors it's far better to erect a proper notice-board somewhere prominent.
- Does this look like the entrance to a thriving, dynamic, learning community in which happy, motivated children are well cared for and where high achievement is the norm?

First impressions – the school entrance

- As you enter the building are you greeted by a smiling face who makes you feel welcome?
- Is the entrance hall (if you've got one) well laid out and attractive? Is there somewhere comfortable to wait? Is there something for you to look at while you wait – perhaps the school brochure, photos of children's activities or a collection of press cuttings from the last school year's events?
- Do you get the feeling of calm industry?
- Are appointments always on time?
- Are your encounters with the staff you meet pleasant and welcoming?

Answer these questions honestly and then make any changes necessary to create a positive, welcoming environment for visitors.

Home-school communications

Many parents' main contact with school is through telephone calls, newsletters, standard letters and other written communications. Whatever the communication it must be of the highest quality.

Telephone communications

- Train yourself and staff to smile when answering the phone. Callers will hear the smile in your voice! Try to sound pleased to hear from the caller, whatever the circumstance

- Liaise with office staff to make sure that the phone never rings more than three times before it is answered – there is nothing worse than being kept waiting on the other end of the line, especially if the caller is a parent who is worried about their child or someone who already has a negative view of the school

- Agree a system for recording all calls including name of caller, time and nature of call, and intended recipient. Ensure that messages are delivered as soon as possible

- Install an answerphone/voicemail but try not to use it between 8.30am and 5.00pm

- If a call is for you, try to take it when it comes in rather than returning it later. If this is not possible, return the call at the first available opportunity, especially if it is from a parent

Home-school communications

Newsletters and other regular communications

Imagine you are the reader of a newsletter/letter from the school. Ask yourself these questions:

- Does the style of this letter make me want to bother with it? Is it attractive and inviting?
- Is it all text or is there a mixture of text, illustration and photographs?
- Is it photocopied straight and accurately on the page? Was the copier working properly at the time, or is the letter blotchy or shadowy?
- Is the information reported positively, or is it just a series of moans and 'don't do's'?
- Are children and their achievements a regular feature of the letter?
- Do I get too many of these?
- How do I know when to expect letters from the school because my child tends to lose them on the way home?

The school shop

Rather than just a cupboard in the school office which contains school uniform and the home/school reading folders, it is possible to create a real school shop fully stocked with a whole range of items which market your school in a positive way.

It needs to be properly organised and run as a small business, all profits from which go into the school.

So who runs the shop?

Your shop could be run by the PTA, by a couple of members of the support staff, parent volunteers or even (as I've seen in some adventurous primary schools where all Year 6 children are given important responsibilities such as this) a committee of responsible Year 6 children.

The school shop

So how does it work?

The following things need to be in place for it to work:

- A designated area needs to be created and turned into a school shop with its own sign, and a price list to be displayed
- Secure storage for stock needs to be provided
- Shopkeepers need to be identified, shown what to do and shown how to do it
- Parents need to know when the shop is open. It is best to identify a regular time and day each week/fortnight throughout the year and stick to it
- All monies need to be transferred into the safe immediately the shop closes
- Shop opening days could be combined with a drop-in coffee morning/afternoon for parents

The school shop

So what does the shop sell?

Ideally, your school shop will carry all the usual stock – uniform, reading folders etc – but it can also sell items which parents would otherwise have to go into town to buy. Importantly, you can gain publicity for your school by making sure that all items sold display the school name and logo.

Consider stocking:

- Leather bookmarks (as sold in National Trust and other outlets)
- Erasers, pencils, pens and pencil cases
- Day-to-day, as well as commemorative, coffee mugs
- Window/car stickers saying things like *'I learned to read at…'* or *'I became a Young Scientist at…'*. Use your imagination to think about what is appropriate for your school
- Various safety items such as cycle helmets or glow-in-the-dark reflectors for clothing or bags

The list is endless but will be determined by what you think is manageable in your own particular school and your own individual circumstances.

Notes

Establishing & Maintaining Credibility

 Good Leadership & Management

 Promoting & Marketing your School

 Efficient, Effective Management Systems

 Staff Welfare

 Motivating & Energising Staff

 Improving Teaching & Learning

 Tips & Further Information

Efficient, Effective Management Systems

Manage yourself before you manage others

Although it's one of the most rewarding and enjoyable jobs you could possibly do, school leadership can be exhausting and difficult, which is why it is so important that you look after yourself properly both personally and professionally. If you aren't firing on all cylinders for most of the time, it's very difficult to maintain the enthusiasm and energy you will require to get everyone else to operate at their own optimum levels.

Looking after your personal needs

- In spite of the huge workload you undoubtedly face, try to find time at least once a week when you are able to do the thing that gives you relief and relaxation away from work. Commit yourself to it and make sure you always do it

- Eat healthily and take regular exercise (yes I know you already know that, but many headteachers fail to make sure they do this)

- Try not to drink too much coffee/tea, but do drink more water

- Try to find one day in the week when you will do no school work at all

Manage yourself before you manage others

Looking after your professional needs

- Go on a time management course
- Go on a project management course
- Equip your office with **everything** you need to do the job. This includes IT equipment, comfortable and appropriate furniture and a direct phone line so you can always make that important call without having to wait for the main external line to be free
- Link up with other heads in your cluster; if there isn't a cluster start one up!
- Make sure you have the right level of office support so that you aren't spending unreasonable amounts of time doing menial things that someone else should be doing

Develop and manage an effective staffing structure

Staff always feel happier if they know exactly what is expected of them.

- Make sure every member of staff has a job description that clearly and unambiguously sets out *concisely* and *precisely* what is expected of them
- Fully involve the member of staff in drawing up their own job description
- Don't make the mistake of omitting important expectations for the sake of being economical with paper
- Have a system to review these at least annually
- Ensure that all staff are aware of each other's roles and responsibilities

Create good communication systems

Teacher stress can be greatly reduced when everyone is kept properly informed about what's going on and when. Spend time creating well laid out, clear systems and procedures for:

- Budget production, profiling, monitoring and management
- Curriculum planning, monitoring and evaluation
- School improvement planning and delivery for staff *and* for governors. Your School Improvement Plan should ideally be tied to the budget plan. Aim to develop a four term SIP which starts in April of one year but finishes in August of the next year, with the following year's plan overlapping in the summer term. Your attached adviser/inspector or headteacher mentor will help and advise.
- Premises management
- Meetings, ie agendas, minutes, record keeping
- Appointments with parents and staff
- Day-to-day office/admin routines – meet regularly with admin staff to discuss issues
- School management and organisational structures

Cut out jargon, so everyone understands exactly what is going on at all times

Create good communication systems

- Produce a staff handbook which sets out your organisational and professional expectations. Allocate responsibility for the handbook to one of your SMT

- Make sure that parents fully understand the school's organisational structure and arrangements by reminding them frequently in newsletters and other communications and by having posters and other informative signs clearly visible around the school. Have these professionally made and go for quality

- Work closely with your chair of governors and clerk to governors to set out guidelines and procedures for all governing body activities. Produce your own 'Governors' Handbook' which includes these procedures as well as terms of reference for each committee and other information you feel governors should have. Introduce the handbook personally as an item at a full governors' meeting and go through it carefully. Spending time at this stage will pay dividends later

Time management – yours and theirs

No matter what their role is in school everyone seems to have too much to do in the time available. Some of this is to do with people not managing their time in the most effective way possible and some of it is to do with genuinely not having enough time!

- Carry out an audit of how much time is wasted in your school, eg waiting for the last class to arrive for assembly, assemblies overrunning, time taken to come in from playtimes, settling down at the start of lessons etc and then do something about it
- Provide time management training for all staff
- Do not allow teachers to be interrupted when they are teaching
- Try not to make sudden and unexpected demands on staff to meet with you – let them know well in advance

Time management – yours and theirs

- Use conditional language to **request** rather than require teachers' time. So, use phrases such as *'Would you mind taking on…'*, rather than *'I want you to take on…'*; *'How would you feel about leading the maths initiative?'*, rather than *'I've decided that you should lead the maths initiative'*; *'Would you have time to meet with me after school today?'* rather than *'I want to see you after school today'*

- Tell people exactly how long a discussion/meeting will take then start and finish meetings on time

- Ensure that your organisational systems allow your teachers to have a proper break as timetabled

- Don't waste your staff's time by holding unnecessary or unproductive meetings or by allowing meetings to contain items which are purely for transmission of information

Project management

Whenever you delegate a task to someone you are effectively asking them to take on a project (large or small) and very few staff have ever had any real training in project management.

In order for them to manage their project effectively they will need to be supported properly. So **either** give them all project management training **or** at least provide them with some in-house guidance on how to manage the task you have delegated to them.

Running successful meetings

Unfortunately, it would be almost impossible to run a school successfully without having a variety of different meetings for different purposes. But if you have to have meetings make sure they are 'NEET'

N	Necessary
E	Effective
E	Efficient
T	Totally Productive

If they aren't, then don't hold them!

Running successful meetings

How to do it:

- Carry out a complete audit of all the meetings regularly held in your school and decide how many of them are *really* needed

- Develop with your SMT an agreed procedure for the organisation and running of all meetings

- Set clear agendas and allow all participants the opportunity to contribute in advance. Agree a closing time and date by which agenda items should be submitted and don't be tempted to be flexible with this. The chair of the meeting should decide how many items can properly be dealt with during any given meeting; don't overload the agenda

- Decide who should attend the meeting and don't expect teachers to attend if they really don't need to be there

Running successful meetings

- Ensure agendas and briefing papers are distributed in enough time to allow participants to absorb the required information

- The chair should arrive well before the meeting begins, and **never** late

- Meetings should begin and end on time, allowing time for any other business (which really should only be items that couldn't possibly have been submitted in time, not items which people just didn't get round to putting on the agenda)

- Appoint a minute-taker for each meeting and ensure that minutes are concise and to the point. Have minutes stored in an organised, easily accessible and chronological way and make sure they are available to everyone who needs them

- Find the time to train your staff on how to run and chair meetings – the time spent on this will be repaid manifold by more successful and more productive meetings throughout the year

Creating the budget

A book like this doesn't pretend to cover everything you need to know about budget management. However there are some basic principles you need to be aware of when planning. The new budget should not suddenly be created in the two or three months prior to April 1st. It should be:

- The result of an ongoing monitoring programme which has taken place throughout the previous year and which informs the decisions you make for the new financial year

- Closely tied to the improvements already highlighted in the School Improvement Plan and based on the submissions already made to you by all those staff who hold budgets

- Based on what you are trying to achieve in your school rather than how much money you have. You should first have prioritised your plans for the new year and costed them all before making any budget decisions. Try to make sure that the high quality education you are aiming to deliver to your children is the top priority for all budget decisions

Generally speaking, it is people rather than things that make the difference, so ensure that after allowing for your fixed costs, funding your staffing needs comes next.

Managing the budget

Once the budget is finalised and agreed with staff and governors it is ready to 'go live'. Managing it during the coming year simply requires you to:

- Delegate responsibility for expenditure to appropriate budget holders
- Put in place a rigorous monitoring programme with your bursar which will ensure that you remain fully in control of all expenditure during the coming year

Managing the premises

Premises management can be a real headache unless you have a good system
in place which helps you to keep on top of things as they develop, rather than when
it's too late. To facilitate this:

- Delegate most of the day-to-day premises monitoring and management to your
  premises manager
- Meet with your premises manager (this need take no longer than ten minutes)
  every week to identify potential problems. Provide him/her with an inspection
  routine and record-keeping system so that all parts of the school are rigorously
  monitored on a regular basis
- Don't use a 'rolling' programme of redecoration – respond to wear and tear as
  needed. Some areas will need redecoration sooner than others owing to heavy
  usage
- Pay particular attention to entrance areas, learning areas, play areas and toilets

What you give you get -
ten times over. So give a
little...
...to everyone,
...every day.

Establishing &
Maintaining
Credibility

 Good
Leadership &
Management

 Promoting &
Marketing your
School

 Efficient, Effective
Management
Systems

 Staff Welfare

 Motivating &
Energising Staff

 Improving
Teaching &
Learning

 Tips & Further
Information

Staff Welfare

Recruiting new staff

The people who will deliver your vision are your staff, so recruiting the right people is crucial to the future success of your school. Although staff recruitment is a complex and time-consuming procedure which needs more space than is available in this book, there is one tip worth remembering when appointing new staff:

Agree with your governors a detailed protocol which reflects your vision and philosophy and sets out specifically and comprehensively your procedures for the recruitment of all staff.

POLICY FOR ADVERTISING, INTERVIEWING AND RECRUITMENT

TEACHING PERSONNEL

Advertising of vacant teaching posts:
- All permanent full-time teaching posts should be advertised nationally
- In an emergency, where time in which an appointment can be made is limited to half a term, then the position need only be advertised locally
- In cases which do not fall into either of the above categories, then a special meeting will be convened
- Headteacher consults on wording of advertisement if appropriate

Recruitment and interviewing procedures:

- The headteacher and chair of the personnel committee will draw up the specific job description, selection criteria and person specification for the post
- Information sent to applicants will include a description of the school and specific details of the vacant post
- All applicants will be invited to arrange a visit to the school
- When shortlisting, the headteacher to consult with the chair of the panel and other members of the committee as appropriate
- The chair of the governing body will be invited to be a member of the interviewing panel
- The headteacher may visit shortlisted applicants in their present post
- Prior to interview, application forms from shortlisted candidates will be circulated to the interview panel
- Members of the interview panel will meet in advance to agree the structure of the interview
- References will only be taken after candidates have completed their interviews
- Interviewed candidates will be informed of the outcome as soon as possible after interviews have been completed
- Debriefing will be offered to unsuccessful candidates
- All applicants will be notified in writing, whether successful or unsuccessful

NON-TEACHING PERSONNEL

Secretarial, clerical, ancillary and caretaking posts will be advertised locally and in the LEA non-teaching bulletin.

Candidates for the posts of secretary, finance assistant and caretaker will be shortlisted and interviewed by the chair, the headteacher plus one other governor from the personnel committee. Applicants for the posts of classroom assistants and cleaners will be shortlisted and interviewed by the headteacher and deputy headteacher

Inducting new staff

New staff (of all categories) join schools all the time. The difficult part is inducting them effectively to help them get up to speed as quickly as possible. Here are some ideas that may help:

- For one afternoon, two or three weeks into every term, free all the new staff who started that term and spend the afternoon with them going through the things you feel are most important for them to get to grips with

- Produce a comprehensive staff handbook, but make sure you give new staff time within their normal working hours to read it through. Include in the handbook clear guidance as to which of the school's major policies it is essential to be familiar with immediately, eg Child Protection, Teaching and Learning, Code of Conduct

- Give new staff the opportunity to work alongside a colleague for the first few days rather than just throwing them in at the deep end. Consider allocating them a mentor for the first year

- Throughout their first term schedule regular meetings for new staff with their line managers to give them the chance to discuss their performance and any other issues which may arise. After the first term these meetings will not be so necessary

Personal needs and emotional support

Do not neglect this important element of staff welfare.

- Greet your staff personally when you see them by using their names. Sound like you're pleased to see them. Give a smile to get a smile!
- Try to talk to staff about their personal lives before engaging in professional discussion. Make a point of remembering individual personal circumstances
- Have a system for remembering birthdays and make a point of mentioning it
- Ensure the staffroom is comfortable, welcoming and meets day-to-day needs
- Play music at the start of meetings to create the right mood
- Offer biscuits/chocolate/fruit occasionally, but **always** at after-school meetings
- Occasionally treat your staff to doughnuts or cakes at morning coffee break

Personal needs and emotional support

- Occasionally (preferably a Friday) arrange for lunchtime supervisors to stay on an extra fifteen minutes to give staff an extended lunch break
- Appoint a toilet refurbishment team and redecorate the staff loos!
- Create reward, recognition and celebration rituals to suit you and your staff
- Be aware that many staff have children of their own and sometimes need your support for a variety of their children's needs
- Be prepared to pay staff to run clubs if you're paying visiting tutors/coaches

Remember the value of a little **give and take**. Be prepared to give your staff days off for special circumstances. If you're flexible they'll repay you threefold with their dedication and commitment. Roll your sleeves up when necessary and get stuck in; join in with activities which teachers would not normally expect to see you doing. Your credibility will increase dramatically.

Personal needs and emotional support

External inspection

One of the most stressful times for staff is when an inspection is due, either from Ofsted or from the LEA. At these times it is important to:

1. Call a meeting with **all** staff as soon as you have been notified of the inspection dates and explain the process to them. Give everyone the chance to ask questions about anything that may be concerning them
2. Agree a timescale for inspection preparation with your SMT and make it public
3. Keep communication channels open so staff are fully up to date with all developments
4. Ensure that everyone receives the support they need to prepare fully for the inspection
5. Don't change direction midstream – stick to your philosophy
6. Don't try to produce policies and documents out of a hat ahead of their scheduled dates for production – this just increases the pressure on staff
7. Seek the involvement of a trusted colleague, headteacher, LEA adviser or external consultant to carry out a pre-inspection audit of your school
8. And finally, when the inspection comes leave your diary **completely** free during that week to be available to support your staff

Professional needs

- Ensure that teachers have all the materials and resources to do the job. Never make them feel that your demands are unreasonable because of lack of resources

- Teachers take great pride in their school. Use the local media to celebrate every worthwhile achievement of your school. Make sure teachers get the recognition they deserve, but stay out of the limelight yourself. This will have a dramatic impact on the perceptions of teachers and parents about their school. It will improve home-school relationships and build teachers' self-esteem

- Every teacher needs to have a clear idea of the chain of command and line management support: where does the buck stop?

- Empower and involve teachers in the day-to-day life of the school. This is one of the most effective ways of raising their self-worth and sense of belonging

- Ensure security of the workforce at all times

Continuing professional development

For effective CPD to take place someone has to have overall responsibility for managing it. This person may be you, but it is probably better for it to be a deputy or assistant head.

- Make sure that your performance management procedures are positive, supportive and developmental. Set objectives that reflect the individual's needs as well as the school's
- Provide all your teachers with access to high quality Inset. Too much time and money is wasted on poor quality training
- Give all your teachers the opportunity to lead professional development sessions, even if it's only a short slot during a staff meeting, but give them some prior training in the skills required. If you can't do that yourself, hire someone else
- Be prepared to respond positively to any request a teacher may make to improve their professionalism, even if it does not fall within their area of responsibility

The staff social committee

Team-building is an essential part of developing a cohesive staff team that is prepared to work for and support each other. You can send everyone off on team-building courses if you wish, but one of the best ways of raising and maintaining morale is by occasionally having social functions together.

- Set up a staff social committee which is representative of **all** the staff. There should be no more than four or five people on it, made up of 'Lawn Mowers' or 'Life Enhancers' but **not** 'Well Poisoners'. Their role is simply to co-ordinate social events through the year, without overdoing it! Sometimes these events will be large, such as the Christmas 'do' or the Easter tenpin bowling trip but just as often they'll be last minute things such as a trip to the pub on a Friday after work

- The committee won't usually need extra time to meet because most arrangements will be made informally, but provide them with it if they do

Establishing & Maintaining Credibility

 Good Leadership & Management

 Promoting & Marketing your School

 Efficient, Effective Management Systems

 Staff Welfare

 Motivating & Energising Staff

 Improving Teaching & Learning

 Tips & Further Information

Motivating & Energising Staff

Understanding motivation

They say that successful schools depend upon three key characteristics in their staff:

Motivation, Motivation, Motivation

But how do we create a highly motivated staff? First we need to understand the motivational loop.

Understanding motivation

People tend to feel motivated when:

- They are doing things they enjoy
- They are trusted with real responsibility – delegate tasks to them
- They are fully supported in their roles
- They have everything they need to carry out their agreed responsibilities
- Their efforts are recognised and celebrated
- They are rewarded when they have achieved

Understanding motivation

The motivational loop – theory

1 Motives
We are motivated to do something

2 Mental Predisposition
Because we are motivated, we develop a positive mental predisposition towards the task

3 Behaviours
Our behaviours change to enable us to achieve our goal

4 Goal
We gain a sense of achievement when we achieve our goal, which makes us want to do more

Achievement

Creating the motivational loop

You will want all your staff to be part of the motivational loop all the time so use the following model for all of them.

The motivational loop – practice

Challenge   Provide each of them with a challenge within their capabilities

Support   Provide them with all the support they need

Recognise   Recognise their achievements as they hit particular milestones

Reward   Reward them in whatever way you think appropriate

Celebrate   Celebrate their achievement

Recognise, reward and celebrate

Recognise

Sometimes a project can take some time to complete. It's important not to wait until completion before recognising the various achievements and milestones passed along the way. Recognition can come in the form of a word from you, a card slipped into a pigeon-hole, a mention to all staff in a staff meeting, or a note of thanks on the staffroom whiteboard. However you recognise people's efforts **while** they are involved in a project, make sure you do!

Reward

Rewarding people for what they have done doesn't necessarily mean a £1000 bonus in the pay packet or two tickets to Jamaica (though that would be nice). For most people the reward is in the journey and the sense of achievement gained upon completion. You will be the best judge of whether or not to formalise the rewards you provide.

Recognise, reward and celebrate

Celebrate, celebrate, celebrate

We all feel good when we have completed a project, so let the whole world know about it! You can celebrate the completion of a major project with a staffroom lunch, involvement of the media, an opening ceremony with invited guests etc. Or you can celebrate quietly with an informal word of thanks to the project leader. You will know what works best with your different members of staff but whatever you do, do something.

Once a project is completed it is important to make sure parents and governors are told about it.

Some daily motivators

Here are some ideas you can use to keep staff morale high and maintain motivational levels:

- When you don't care, they don't care. Show you care
- Give credit where it's due – every day
- Challenge all prejudice
- Use positive language at all times
- When someone does something really well, pen a note to their line manager
- Praise progress as well as results
- Pay as much attention to your most junior member of staff as you do to your most senior member of staff

Some daily motivators

- Notice when staff do what they are expected to do and tell them. Try to avoid only noticing when they don't do what they are expected to do
- If **you** can do it **I** can do it. Foster a 'can-do' spirit in the way you talk to your staff
- The person who never made a mistake never made anything. Recognise and reward risk-taking, innovation and creativity
- Enthusiasm is infectious, so be enthusiastic
- No one can do everything but everyone can do something – help all your staff to believe in themselves by giving them your support
- Do it now
- Always choose quality over quantity

Some daily motivators

- Ask rather than tell
- Give every employee a personal goal which will benefit both the school and them
- Delete *'but'* from your vocabulary
- Smile
- Remember to say thank you to those who are going about their daily tasks for the good of the school and the children
- It doesn't really matter that you fall; what matters is what you do when you get up
- The best way to get respect and responsibility from your staff is to give it to them in the first place

Some daily energisers

- Do something special for one employee – today, and do that for a different employee every day
- Have a space made available in the staff-room for people to display humorous newspaper articles, jokes or pictures
- Once a term provide a special breakfast for staff before they begin work
- Give out humorous certificates of recognition to acknowledge individual achievements
- Make a point of talking to those staff you interact with least
- Invite some of the most junior members of staff to have lunch with you

Some daily energisers

- Send a problem that you are personally grappling with to all staff and ask them to give you suggestions on how to solve it
- Create a staff suggestion box – and act on the suggestions made
- When others are in crisis be calm and decisive
- Pay people compliments; flattery gets you everywhere!
- Break the rules sometimes
- Use affirmation posters in the staffroom and around the school with statements like, *'Problems are just opportunities in disguise'* and, *'If you don't know where you're going, any road will take you there'*.
- Recognise people when they use initiative

Establishing &
Maintaining
Credibility

 Good
Leadership &
Management

 Promoting &
Marketing your
School

 Efficient, Effective
Management
Systems

 Staff Welfare

 Motivating &
Energising Staff

 Improving
Teaching &
Learning

 Tips & Further
Information

Improving Teaching & Learning

Philosophy – what's yours?

> Children come to school to play
> and to see their friends
>
> (we think they come to school to learn!)

Children don't choose to come to school – they just find that that's where they are for 190 days every year because their parents send them!

Philosophy – what's yours?

If you ask any young child what they did at school on any given day, the inevitable answer is often something like *'nothing'* or *'not much'*. However, if you change the question and ask *'Who did you play with today?'* you're more likely to get a response, because in the mind of a young child the things that most matter are:

(a) that they have friends (and that all of us are their friends)

and

(b) that their time in school (both in class and during playtimes) feels like play, because play is what inspires and motivates them

It's important that we understand this because if we are to provide a learning environment in which every child can really thrive, we must understand how they think about school and what really motivates them. Our philosophy needs to be founded on a clear understanding of how children learn, and every decision we make regarding their education should be based on that understanding.

Philosophy – what's yours?

We want our children to be leaping out of their beds in the morning because they are coming into our school and they know that the whole day is going to be a wonderfully rewarding and magical learning journey which they won't want to end. Does that sound like your school? Here's how you can make a start on creating that kind of environment for your children:

- Through lengthy and full consultation with **all** your staff, produce a detailed Teaching and Learning Policy which sets out your agreed expectations in every aspect of teaching and learning in your school. Your own expectations should come through loud and clear

- Through lengthy and full consultation with **all** your staff, produce a detailed Code of Behaviour (linked very closely to your PSHE Policy) which is 95% positive reward and affirmation and 5% sanction

Philosophy – what's yours?

- Concentrate on providing the highest quality Inset for your staff. Avoid low quality but apparently necessary input recommended by LEA inspectors/advisers and others who don't necessarily share your philosophy!

- Put in place a comprehensive monitoring programme which ensures that you are always aware of what's going on in the classroom

- Aim to raise standards, not by spending all your energies on hitting ridiculous and meaningless summative targets, but by creating the kind of learning environment in which children are so highly motivated, so happy, so eager to learn and are provided with such a rich, broad-based curriculum that they are truly inspired. You'll find they just can't help achieving standards that others thought were unachievable!

Philosophy – what's yours?

Deciding your approach

National Curriculum testing at the end of Key Stage 1 and 2 is a fact of life in the primary school. Although you may not want to do the tests, you may as well give your children the best chance to do as well as they can when the tests arrive, so:

- Prepare them fully for the test situation by administering a few 'mock' tests beforehand
- Try not to sacrifice everything in Year 6 in order to 'drill' the children for the tests – children learn best when they are exposed to variety, inspiration and multi-sensory learning
- Teach children memory techniques from three years old and upwards
- Teach children memory mapping techniques and use them throughout your school
- Don't pressurise the children by allowing staff to make constant reference to 'Levels' being achieved
- Try to avoid Year 2 and Year 6 homework activities being all SATs related

Accelerated learning

One of the best ways to improve the quality of teaching and learning is to introduce accelerated learning techniques into your school. Although there is not space here to explain this in detail, the following will provide a starting point:

- Create an emotionally supportive learning environment
- Develop an understanding of the physiological and psychological needs of children as learners
- Start lessons in a positive, prompt way and finish by recapping the learning
- Deliver the key learning points using a multi-sensory approach to include visual, auditory and kinaesthetic (VAK) stimuli
- Build in regular concentration breaks
- Use formative assessment and positive feedback

The bibliography on pages 124-125 suggests ideas for further reading.

The importance of good Inset

It is vital both to appoint high quality staff and then to provide them with the best possible CPD you can afford. Although it is sometimes necessary to send staff out on courses for their own individual development, the best way to improve teaching and learning across the entire school is through whole-school Inset. Try to take account of these principles when planning this kind of training for your staff:

- If one of your staff is to deliver the Inset themselves, make sure they have all the necessary skills to inspire and motivate others and to present the key elements of the day in a stimulating, enjoyable way

- If you do not have someone on your staff who can deliver what you want, don't penny-pinch by hiring someone else on the cheap if you are not **certain** of their capabilities. Whatever the cost, hire the person who is best known (and most likely to be inspirational) in that particular field

The importance of good Inset

- If the event is to be held in school, the day will run more smoothly if one person (not the person delivering the Inset) has specific responsibility for all domestic arrangements ie coffee/tea, lunch, etc

- If the budget will stretch to it, take the staff out to a local conference venue rather than stay on school premises – it lends greater importance to the event and makes people feel valued

- Build in time in one or two subsequent staff meetings to follow up what was covered on the day

- Summarise what has been agreed, make sure this summary reaches **everyone** who needs to know, then monitor the newly agreed changes to practice during the next six to nine months

Monitoring

There's no point in having the best teaching and learning policy in the world if there isn't a monitoring programme in place to ensure that the policy is working in practice. Your programme should aim to ensure high quality planning, excellent delivery of the agreed curriculum, and outcomes which reflect your expectations and shared vision.

Your monitoring programme should be:

- Manageable:
  – **You** don't have to monitor everything. Your subject leaders should be monitoring individual subject areas – you and your deputy/assistant head should be monitoring overall quality of teaching and learning

  – Set out a monitoring programme for the whole year in September and then publicise it to all who need to know

- Rigorous and comprehensive
- Supportive, developmental and not overly critical

Monitoring

Planning

Many headteachers think that they need to see teachers' plans every week – you don't. The important thing is that you see them enough to let you know that the agreed content of your curriculum is being delivered.

- Tie in the scrutiny of a teacher's planning file with the occasion of their lesson observation and the scrutiny of their pupils' work. That way you can see the whole process of planning, delivery and outcomes all in one go
- Encourage your teachers to plan more 'smartly' by avoiding pages of narrative and using bullet points more effectively
- Devise a system of (positive and supportive) feedback so that you can let teachers know what you think of their planning
- Return planning files as soon as the monitoring is over

Monitoring

Lesson observations

One of the most important things you can do to improve children's learning is to watch teachers teaching. Obvious isn't it? Your lesson observation programme should ensure that you see every teacher teach at least twice every year (more where there is a concern) but it should also:

- Reflect the stated expectations in your teaching and learning policy
- Provide teachers with **immediate** positive feedback on their teaching (see next page for suggested possible format for lesson observations)
- Aim to cover the whole curriculum, not just the core areas
- Lead by example and occasionally let teachers observe **you** teach!

The table opposite identifies the characteristics you might look for when carrying out a lesson observation.

Monitoring

Lesson observations

Planning	◁ Poor			Excellent ▷
Clear learning intentions are evident				
VAK* is planned to be used				
Differentiation by task, outcome or delivery is noted				
Concentration breaks are planned				

Primacy				
Children settle quickly and are ready to learn promptly				
Lesson begins with a connecting activity if appropriate				
Differentiation by delivery is used if necessary				
Classroom furniture is organised appropriately and materials are readily available				
Multi-sensory input is used				
Information is delivered concisely and with enthusiasm, creating interest in the children				

* Visual, Auditory, Kinaesthetic.

Monitoring

Lesson observations

Main Part of the Lesson	◁ Poor		Excellent ▷		
Children know what to do					
Activities are appropriate for all children					
Concentration breaks occur as appropriate					
Formative assessment is used, feedback is positive					
Praise and encouragement are used generously					

Recency					
Plenary activity involves all the children, is fun and leaves children on a high as the lesson ends – on time					

Additional Characteristics					
Music is used for a particular purpose					
Tone of voice and body language are encouraging and supportive					
Discipline is maintained					
Children are on task throughout the lesson					
Questioning engages all children					
Children enjoy what they are doing					

Monitoring

Scrutiny of children's work

You can scrutinise children's work in a number of different ways, but the key thing is to find out as much as you can about how they are doing. Subject leaders should already be monitoring standards in their own subjects and leaving you and the deputy to concentrate on overall achievement. Try this method of work scrutiny:

- In the same week you are to carry out one of your formal lesson observations ask for three children (top, middle and bottom) from that class to be sent to you with **all** the work they have done so far this year

- Give children a chance to chat informally to you about their favourite lesson/day/activity before asking them questions

Monitoring

Scrutiny of children's work

- Devise a series of questions which will give you information about how they are being taught, eg *'How does your teacher help you when you are stuck?'*, *'How do you know what you are going to learn each day?'* etc. These questions should be known in advance by the teacher being observed, having been devised at the beginning of the school year and shared with all staff. Use the same questions every time you scrutinise children's work

- One of you asks the questions, the other makes notes (on the computer) and prepares a summary which goes straight to the teacher as part of their feedback at the end of their lesson observation. Feedback should be positive and developmental

Establishing &
Maintaining
Credibility

 Good
Leadership &
Management

 Promoting &
Marketing your
School

 Efficient, Effective
Management
Systems

 Staff Welfare

 Motivating &
Energising Staff

 Improving
Teaching &
Learning

 Tips & Further
Information

Tips & Further
Information

Tips and Further Information

1. Model the behaviours you expect of others
2. Live the message you espouse
3. Set the standard and keep to it
4. Only do what only you can do
5. Listen more than you talk
6. Manage yourself before you manage others
7. Treat your staff as people first and staff second
8. Start each day positively and cheerfully – and stay there
9. Start and finish meetings on time
10. Develop excellent systems, strategies and procedures before anything else

9. Start and finish meetings on time
10. Develop excellent systems, strategies and procedures before anything else
11. Create a 'High Challenge, Low Stress' atmosphere in your school
12. Use staff's first names at the start of every conversation
13. Constantly revisit (with your staff) the school's vision, or parts of it. Remind everyone what it is you are collectively trying to achieve
14. Create a positive emotionally supportive environment
15. Create a positive working environment
16. Be decisive and consistent
17. Be aware of the differing motivational levels of your teachers and do something about it!
18. In every situation think 'Win/Win'
19. There's no such thing as a problem – just a situation that needs a decision and a solution, so make the decision and find the solution
20. Happiness, humour and personal well-being are infectious – so SMILE!!

Further reading: leadership and management

The Competent Manager: A Model for Effective Performance by Richard E. Boyatzis Published by John Wiley and Sons, New York (1982)

The Emotionally Intelligent Workplace: How to Select for, Measure and Improve Emotional Intelligence in Individuals, Groups and Organizations Ed. Cary Cherniss, Daniel Goleman Published by Jossey-Bass Wiley (2001)

The 7 Habits of Highly Effective People by Stephen R. Covey Published by Simon & Schuster (1999)

Effective Leadership for School Improvement by Alma Harris et al Published by Routledge Falmer (2002)

School Improvement for Real by David Hopkins Published by Routledge Falmer (2001)

Human Motivation by D.C. McClelland Published by Schott, Foresman & Co., Illinois (1988)

Further reading: teaching and learning

Accelerated Learning Pocketbook **by Brin Best**
Published by Teachers' Pocketbooks (2003)

Becoming Emotionally Intelligent **by Catherine Corrie**
Published by Network Educational Press (2003)

Smart Moves **by Carla Hannaford**
Published by Great Ocean Publishers (1995)

The Learning to Learn Pocketbook by Tom Barwood
Published by Teachers' Pocketbooks (2005)

Closing the Learning Gap **by Mike Hughes**
Published by Network Educational Press (1999)

Bringing the Best Out in Boys **by Lucinda Neall**
Published by Hawthorn Press (2003)

Accelerated Learning in Practice **by Alistair Smith**
Published by Network Educational Press (1998, 2nd edition)

The ALPS Approach **by Alistair Smith & Nicola Call**
Published by Network Educational Press (1999 – revised 2000)

Some useful websites

Leadership and management

www.ncsl.org	school leadership
www.primarytrans.com	primary school leadership
www.teachernet.gov.uk	school leadership
www.ioe.ac.uk	school leadership – research
www.pocketbook.co.uk	books on leadership/management

Teaching and learning

www.alite.co.uk	accelerated learning
www.musica.uci.edu	music and learning
www.uea.ac.uk	teacher characteristics
www.casel.org	emotional intelligence
www.nlp-cds.co.uk	neuro-linguistic programming
www.primarytrans.com	all teaching and learning
www.dana.org	brain research
www.teacherspocketbooks.co.uk	books on a range of topics

About the author

Bruce Potts

Author Bruce Potts has extensive experience in infant, junior and primary schools over a period of 25 years. A former primary headteacher who has turned around a failing inner city and a village school, he now mentors new headteachers, has led a variety of school/community projects as director of an EAZ and, as an independent education consultant and trainer, is widely known for his inspirational and motivational work in the field of teaching & learning and leadership & management.

Bruce would be happy to help you develop any of the ideas mentioned in this book in your own school. He can be contacted through his website: www.primarytrans.com.

Order Form

Your details

Name _____

Position _____

School _____

Address _____

_____

_____

Telephone _____

Fax _____

E-mail _____

VAT No. (EC only) _____

Your Order Ref _____

Please send me:

		No. copies
Primary Headteacher's	Pocketbook	☐
_____	Pocketbook	☐
_____	Pocketbook	☐
_____	Pocketbook	☐
_____	Pocketbook	☐

Order by Post

**Teachers'
Pocketbooks**

Laurel House, Station Approach
Alresford, Hants. SO24 9JH UK

Order by Phone, Fax or Internet

Telephone: +44 (0)1962 735573
Facsimile: +44 (0)1962 733637
E-mail: sales@teacherspocketbooks.co.uk
Web: www.teacherspocketbooks.co.uk